4890 2455

Night animals

Bobbie Kalman

 Crabtree Publishing Company

www.crabtreebooks.com

Created by Bobbie Kalman

Author and Editor-in-Chief
Bobbie Kalman

Educational consultants
Elaine Hurst
Joan King
Jennifer King

Notes for adults
Jennifer King

Editors
Kathy Middleton
Crystal Sikkens

Design
Bobbie Kalman
Katherine Berti

Print and production coordinator
Katherine Berti

Prepress technician
Katherine Berti

Photo research
Bobbie Kalman

Photographs
Bat Conservation International: ©Merlin D. Tuttle:
    page 9
Other photographs by Shutterstock

Library and Archives Canada Cataloguing in Publication

Kalman, Bobbie, 1947-
    Night animals / Bobbie Kalman.

(My world)
Issued also in electronic format.
ISBN 978-0-7787-9558-2 (bound).--ISBN 978-0-7787-9583-4 (pbk.)

    1. Nocturnal animals--Juvenile literature. I. Title. II. Series:
My world (St. Catharines, Ont.)

QL755.5.K34 2011   j591.5'18   C2010-907436-X

Library of Congress Cataloging-in-Publication Data

Kalman, Bobbie.
 Night animals / Bobbie Kalman.
    p. cm. -- (My world)
 ISBN 978-0-7787-9583-4 (pbk. : alk. paper) -- ISBN 978-0-7787-9558-2
(reinforced library binding : alk. paper) -- ISBN 978-1-4271-9665-1
(electronic (pdf))
 1. Nocturnal animals--Juvenile literature. I. Title.
 QL755.5.K35 2011
 591.5'18--dc22

                                    2010047122

Crabtree Publishing Company
www.crabtreebooks.com   1-800-387-7650

Printed in China/022011/RG20101116

Published in Canada
Crabtree Publishing
616 Welland Ave.
St. Catharines, Ontario
L2M 5V6

Published in the United States
Crabtree Publishing
PMB 59051
350 Fifth Avenue, 59th Floor
New York, New York 10118

Published in the United Kingdom
Crabtree Publishing
Maritime House
Basin Road North, Hove
BN41 1WR

Published in Australia
Crabtree Publishing
386 Mt. Alexander Rd.
Ascot Vale (Melbourne)
VIC 3032

Words to know

bat

daytime

firefly

light

fox

insect

night

nocturnal

owl

raccoon

senses

Night animals have strong **senses** that help them find food at night. They sleep in the **daytime**.
Owls are night animals.
This owl is sleeping in the daytime.

Big eyes and good hearing help owls find food in the dark.

These owls have found **insects** to eat.

Raccoons are night animals.
They sleep in the daytime.
This raccoon is sleeping in a tree.

Raccoons have special eyes
that help them see at night.
Their eyes seem to glow in the dark.

Bats are night animals.
They hunt insects at night.

Bats have special hearing that helps them find food in the dark. This way of hearing helps them hunt for insects and other animals to eat.

Fireflies are night animals.
They can make their own **light**.
Small insects come to the light,
and the firefly eats them.

This frog sees the light
of the firefly.
Will it eat the firefly?

Foxes hunt at night
or in the daytime.
They sleep in the daytime, but
they sometimes sleep at night.

This fox is sleeping at night.
Which other animals sleep at night?
Turn the page to see if you know!

Activity

Night animals are called **nocturnal** animals.

Which of these animals are nocturnal?

Which animals do you see in the daytime?

raccoon

bat

squirrel

fox

chipmunk

Night animals
bat, raccoon, fox

Day animals
squirrel, fox, chipmunk

Notes for adults

Objective
- to learn the habits of nocturnal animals
- to identify diurnal and nocturnal animals
- to identify strong senses in animals
- to use word study to identify long and short vowel sounds in the book

Before reading
Ask the children to think about the habits of their pets.
"Do you have a pet?"
"What does it do during the day?"
"What does it do at night?"

Questions after reading the book
"What are your five senses?"
"Do night animals have special senses?"
"What are the strongest senses of owls?" (big eyes, good hearing)
"What is special about the eyes of raccoons?" (Their eyes glow in the dark.)
"How do bats find insects in the dark?" (Echolocation—they send out sounds that come back to them as echoes, telling them where prey is.)
"How do fireflies use their light?" (They attract insects with them.)
"How can the light of fireflies work against them?" (They can also attract predators, such as frogs.)

Word power
Have the children identify and practice long and short vowel sounds. Then ask them to write some words containing these vowel sounds on chart paper to hang up in the class.
Long: eyes, tree, fireflies, bright
Short: fox, bat, frog, hunt

Collage center!
Set up six centers with one animal cut out and one trait (which is key in identifying the animal) at each center. The children will glue the special trait onto the animal's picture. Examples: big eyes for owls, glowing eyes for raccoons, bright body light for fireflies

Extension
Prepare pre-cut pictures of the animals from the book along with other animals (nocturnal and diurnal). Discuss how the day animals and night animals are alike and different.
Model for children:
Owls and raccoons are alike because... (They both have special eyes for seeing at night, and they both sleep during the day.)
Bats and foxes are different because... (Bats do not hunt during the day.)

For teacher's guide, go to www.crabtreebooks.com/teachersguides